TROMBONE

C0-APE-207

ISBN 0-634-00587-1

HAL•LEONARD® CORPORATION

7777 W. BLUEMOUND RD. P.O. BOX 13819 MILWAUKEE, WI 53213

Visit Hal Leonard Online at
www.halleonard.com

BOOGIE WOOGIE BUGLE BOY

from BUCK PRIVATES

Words and Music by
DON RAYE and HUGHIE PRINCE

TROMBONE

GO DADDY-O

Words and Music by
SCOTTY MORRIS

IN THE MOOD

By JOE GARLAND

TROMBONE

IT DON'T MEAN A THING

(If It Don't Got That Swing)

from SOPHISTICATED LADIES

TROMBONE

Words and Music by
DUKE ELLINGTON and IRVING MILLS

JUMP, JIVE AN' WAIL

Words and Music by
LOUIS PRIMA

TROMBONE

JUMPIN' JACK

Words and Music by
SCOTTY MORRIS

TROMBONE

LEAP FROG

Music by JOE GARLAND

TROMBONE

PUTTIN' ON THE RITZ

from the Motion Picture PUTTIN' ON THE RITZ

Words and Music by
IRVING BERLIN

TROMBONE

STOMPIN' AT THE SAVOY

TROMBONE

By BENNY GOODMAN,
EDGAR SAMPSON and CHICK WEBB

WHEN I CHANGE YOUR MIND

Words and Music by
STEVE PERRY

TROMBONE

WOODCHOPPER'S BALL

By JOE BISHOP
and WOODY HERMAN

TROMBONE

YOU & ME

Words and Music by
SCOTTY MORRIS

TROMBONE

YOU'RE THE BOSS

Words and Music by
JERRY LEIBER and MIKE STOLLER

TROMBONE

ZOOT SUIT RIOT

Words and Music by
STEVE PERRY

TROMBONE